Comparing
People From
the Past

Mary Seacole,
Florence Nightingale
and Edith Cavell

Nick Hunter

raintree

a Capstone company — publishers for children

Raintree is an imprint of Capstone Global Library Limited, a company incorporated in England and Wales having its registered office at 7 Pilgrim Street, London, EC4V 6LB – Registered company number: 669558

www.raintreepublishers.co.uk
myorders@raintreepublishers.co.uk

Text © Capstone Global Library Limited 2015
The moral rights of the proprietor have been asserted.

Edited by Clare Lewis and Linda Staniford
Designed by Philippa Jenkins
Original illustrations © Capstone Global Library Ltd 2015
Illustrated by HL Studios, Witney, Oxon
Picture research by Gina Kammer
Production by Victoria Fitzgerald
Originated by Capstone Global Library Ltd
Printed and bound in China

ISBN 978 1 406 28991 6
19 18 17 16 15
11 10 9 8 7 6 5 4 3

British Library Cataloguing in Publication Data
A full catalogue record for this book is available from the British Library.

Acknowledgements
We would like to thank the following for permission to reproduce photographs: Alamy: ARGO Images/Nightingale Archive, 14, Everett Collection Historical, 19, The Print Collector, 24; Bridgeman Images: © Look and Learn/Private Collection/Edith Cavell being arrested, Dear, Neville (b.1923), 23, Giraudon/Bibliotheque Nationale, Paris, France/Sister Victoire Darras tending the cholera victims at the Hotel-Dieu of Chauny, 1832 (litho) (b/w photo), Thomas, Napoleon (19th century) (after), 5, Prismatic Pictures/Private Collection/Hospital in Berlin, 1945 (photo), 26, Private Collection/Cover of the first edition of 'The Wonderful Adventures of Mrs Seacole', published by James Blackwood of Paternoster Row, 1857 (engraving) (b/w photo), English School, (19th century), 25, Private Collection/Our Own Vivandiere, Mrs Seacole (1805-81) as depicted in 'Punch', published 20th May 1857 (engraving) (b/w photo), English School, (19th century), 21; Corbis: Hulton-Deutsch Collection, 16; Crialmages.com/Jay Robert Nash Collection, 17; Getty Images: De Agostini Picture Library/DEA PICTURE LIBRARY, 10, Popperfoto, 7, Science Faction/Library of Congress, 28; Glow Images: Heritage Images/The Print Collector, 29 (left), cover (left); HL Studios, 20, 22; Mary Evans Picture Library, 29 (right); National Portrait Gallery, London, 6; Newscom: Mirrorpix/Collect, 12, World History Archive, 4, 8, 18; North Wind Picture Archives: 11, 13, 15; Norwich Castle Museum & Art Gallery (detail): cover (right); Shutterstock: Everett Collection, 9, KavardakovA, cover (background), 1, Sandy Stupart, 27, Bridgeman Art Library, London, cover (middle).

Every effort has been made to contact copyright holders of material reproduced in this book. Any omissions will be rectified in subsequent printings if notice is given to the publisher.

Contents

Some words are shown in bold, **like this.** You can find out what they mean by looking in the glossary.

Who was Florence Nightingale?

Florence Nightingale was the most famous nurse in history. Her fame spread after she cared for injured soldiers during the Crimean War (1854–1856). Nightingale's work changed nursing forever.

Nightingale helped to make hospitals better for everyone.

Early Victorian hospitals were often crowded, dirty and dangerous.

Nightingale worked during the **Victorian** Age. This was a time of change in society. People were starting to understand how diseases spread and find new ways to care for the sick.

Who was Mary Seacole?

Mary Seacole also cared for wounded soldiers during the Crimean War. She was born in Jamaica, which was part of the **British Empire**. Mary's father was Scottish and her mother was from Jamaica.

This is the only **portrait** of Seacole painted during her lifetime.

In Mary Seacole's time, there were fewer black people in Britain than there are today. This is a photo from a school taken during the time when she was alive.

Seacole spent much of her life in Britain. She thought of herself as being British. When Seacole came to Britain, only a few thousand black people lived there.

Who was Edith Cavell?

Edith Cavell tended the sick in World War I. Cavell was born in Norfolk, England in 1865. She trained nurses in Belgium. When war broke out there in 1914, Cavell wanted to help the injured soldiers.

This picture shows Cavell, with her two dogs, before the war.

More people were killed and injured in World War I than in any previous war.

Cavell had a deep **Christian** faith. She believed that she should help everyone that she could. Her beliefs were strongly tested in World War I.

Where did they grow up?

Florence came from a wealthy family. They had servants, like many rich **Victorian** families. Florence and her sister did not go to school. Their father taught them at home.

Florence spent her childhood with her older sister, Frances.

We don't know if Mary went to school. She loved to play at nursing. As a young girl, she helped her mother to nurse sick soldiers. She made the long voyage to Britain when she was fifteen.

Edith grew up in a village in Norfolk. Her father was the vicar of the local church. Edith, her sisters and brother were not rich. They were taught to share what they had with others.

As a young woman, Edith loved art and nature.

Edith was sent to a **boarding school** where she learned to speak French. She worked as a **governess** for children of wealthy families. In 1890, Edith moved to Brussels, Belgium to work for a family there.

How did they become nurses?

Nightingale's family were unhappy about her plan to be a nurse. Rich young ladies were supposed to get married, not work in dirty hospitals. Nightingale had to go to Germany for training.

Nightingale was determined that she would be able to help others.

Seacole's mother taught her to use plants and herbs as medicines. Together they ran a hotel, or hospital, to care for sick soldiers. In 1836 Mary married Edwin Seacole but he died in 1844.

Cavell decided to become a nurse after caring for her sick father. She trained as a nurse in London. The work was badly paid and nurses worked long hours.

Cavell spent her first years as a nurse in British hospitals.

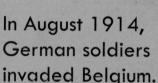

In August 1914, German soldiers invaded Belgium.

In 1907, Cavell returned to Brussels to train other nurses. Cavell learned from Florence Nightingale's ideas on caring for patients. While visiting Norfolk in 1914, she learned that war had broken out.

What did they do to help in wartime?

In 1854, British and French troops went to fight the Crimean War in southern Russia. Medical care was terrible. Nightingale was asked to lead a team of nurses in Scutari, Turkey.

Many soldiers in the Crimean War suffered illness, as well as the risk of injury in battle.

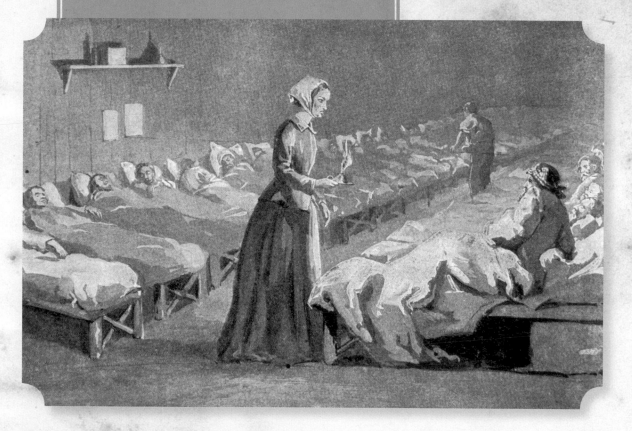

The nurses discovered a filthy hospital overrun with rats. Wounded soldiers were dying of disease in the overcrowded wards. Nightingale made sure that her patients had clean wards, good food and care.

Seacole wanted to help in the Crimean War too. Although the army turned her down, she went anyway. She met Nightingale on the way.

This map shows the area where the Crimean War was fought.

Seacole set up a hotel close to the battlefields. The hotel was more like a hut. Seacole provided hot food, drinks, clothes and rest for the wounded and exhausted soldiers. They called her Mother Seacole.

Cavell worked for the **Red Cross** in Belgium, caring for the wounded of all sides. Belgium was controlled by Britain's enemy, Germany. Cavell helped prisoners from Britain and its **allies** to escape.

Cavell helped soldiers to escape to the Netherlands, which was not involved in the war.

Cavell knew that by helping others she was in danger herself.

On 31 July 1915, Cavell was arrested. She bravely admitted helping soldiers to escape. The punishment for helping Germany's enemies was death. Cavell was executed on 12 October 1915.

What happened after the war?

After the Crimean War, Nightingale was famous. She worked for the rest of her life, training nurses and fighting for better conditions in hospital. She was called the "mother of modern nursing".

In later life, Nightingale was often ill. All her hard work to make nursing better affected her own health.

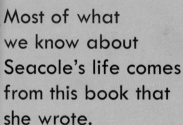

Most of what we know about Seacole's life comes from this book that she wrote.

Seacole also became famous. Soldiers told people about the care she had given them in the war. Her work in the war had left her very poor. People raised money to help her stay in London.

How did times change during their lives?

When Nightingale and Seacole were born, medical care was very basic. They both improved the lives of their patients. Their work also changed nursing for everyone else.

After the work of Nightingale and Seacole, hospitals were much cleaner and nurses were better trained.

This statue helps people to remember Cavell's life and her courage.

By 1919, Cavell's body was returned to Britain. The world was recovering from a terrible war. Millions of soldiers had been killed. Cavell's courage made her a heroine of the war.

Comparing Florence Nightingale,

Florence Nightingale

Born
12 May 1820

Died
13 August 1910

Background
Came from a rich family and chose to be a nurse against her family's wishes

War experience
Ran a hospital in Turkey during the Crimean War

Famous people living at the same time

- Louis Pasteur (scientist who explained how diseases are caused, 1822–1895)
- Isambard Kingdom Brunel (engineer, 1806–1859)
- Charles Dickens (writer, 1812–1870)

FLORENCE NIGHTINGALE

MARY SEACOLE

1800   1850

Mary Seacole and Edith Cavell

Mary Seacole

Born
1805

Died
14 May 1881

Background
Grew up in Jamaica and learned nursing skills from her mother

War experience
Ran the British Hotel for soldiers near the battlefield in the Crimean War

Famous people living at the same time
• Edward Jenner (scientist who discovered vaccination, 1749–1823)

Edith Cavell

Born
4 December 1865

Died
12 October 1915

Background
Came from a religious family, and always wanted to help others

War experience
Was a **Red Cross** nurse in Belgium during World War I (1914–1918)

Famous people living at the same time
• Emmeline Pankhurst (campaigner for women's rights, 1858–1928)

EDITH CAVELL

1900

1950

Glossary

allies friends or countries that fight on the same side in a war

boarding school school where pupils live rather than going home every day

British Empire area of land around the world ruled over by Great Britain. This empire was biggest during the Victorian Age.

Christian believing in Christianity, a religion based on the teachings of Jesus Christ

governess woman who teaches and looks after children in a private household

portrait picture of a person

Red Cross international organization that helps people in crisis or during war

Victorian during the time of Queen Victoria, who ruled Britain from 1837 until 1901

Find out more

Books

Florence Nightingale (History Makers), Sarah Ridley (Franklin Watts, 2013)

Who was Mary Seacole?, Paul Harrison (Wayland, 2009)

Women in World War I, Nick Hunter (Raintree, 2013)

Victorian Health, Fiona MacDonald (Franklin Watts, 2009)

Websites

www.bbc.co.uk/programmes/p015j6sc
Watch this video recreation of Florence Nightingale's life.

www.maryseacole.com
This website tells the remarkable story of Mary Seacole.

www.revdc.net/cavell/
Visit this website to discover more about the life of Edith Cavell.

Index

British Empire 6

Cavell, Edith 8–9, 12–13,
    16–17, 22–23, 27, 29
Christian faith 9
Crimean War 3, 4, 6, 18–
    21

diseases 5, 19

execution 23

fame 24, 25

governesses 13

hospitals 4, 5, 14, 15, 19,
    24, 26
hotels 15, 21

medicines 15

Nightingale, Florence 4–5,
    10, 14, 17, 18–19, 20,
    24, 26, 28
nursing 4–5, 8, 11, 14–17,
    18–19, 21, 22, 24, 26

prisoner escapes 22

Red Cross 22

schools 7, 13
Seacole, Mary 6–7, 11, 15,
    20–21, 25, 26, 29

training 8, 14, 16, 17, 24,
    26

Victorian Age 5

World War I 8–9, 17, 22–
    23, 27